MW01232026

WHEN THE STARS GO DARK

poems by

Jim McGarrah

MAIN STREET RAG PUBLISHING COMPANY
CHARLOTTE, NORTH CAROLINA

Acknowledgements:

Cafe Review: "In Memorium: Hunter S. Thompson"
North American Review: "Operation Lancaster"
Elixir Magazine: "Suicide," "Anghiari," "Peeling Potatoes,"
    "Guernic"
Vilenica International Literary Anthology: "Two Love Poems"
Open 24 Hours: "Cycles," "Generation Gap Redux"
Poetry Southeast: "On the Fiftieth Anniversary of Murder in
    Mississippi..."
Re)Verb Magazine: "Metaphor," "Lesbian Sox"
Unbound Magazine: "March is the Cruelest Month,"
    "Dia Des Muertos," "Last Night at the Gibson
    County Fair"
Poems of Recovery Anthology: "Peace"

With Gratitude

*Thanks to many friends who helped edit these poems, especially
Ron Mitchell, MatthewGraham, David Bartholomy, Brittney
Scott, David Siegel, and Michael Waters.*

Main Street Rag
PO Box 690100
Charlotte, NC 28227
www.MainStreetRag.com

To Bart, who started it all

Contents

II

PROLOGUE:
In Memoriam: Hunter S. Thompson

Time held me green and dying
though I sang in chains like the sea.
—Dylan Thomas

After all, it was HST not JFK, so I graded freshman essays
the day he put a bullet through his cruel, drug-crazed gonzo genius,

and sipped bourbon from a square glass while birds and barren trees
mocked the passing of a generation that wanted to get life right

but never did, that fought a war then fought a war to end the war,
that blessed and cursed itself as caretaker of its own mortality.

Then, I imagined Hunter alone, the wind lifting the skirt of his mind
to expose his hope, numbed and withered by the constant wash

of chemicals through his addled blood, his hope that if misery fuels
self-destruction, then so must love. You know, the kind of love

forcing children to stick their hands in beehives and grope for honey,
driving men to wander river banks late at night, counting stars, listening

as the waves from coal barges break over frozen stones on the cut bank
in the warm rhythm of a young woman's heartbeat, the kind of love

that brings a boy to the front of a moving tank in Tiananmen Square,
a girl to give up her child, a soldier to fall on a grenade, the feeling

hidden in us all that something exists somewhere more worthy
than the self. This is what finally killed Hunter Thompson, not bullets,

not drugs, not even the indifference of new generations. It's the same
cross that Jesus chose to hang on, the same need to fuel the myth

of love that grants us grace beyond our own humanity, if only in shadows,
like a moonflower opens its petals and bears its soul to the darkness.

I

*In the year 2004, Dark Energy
is Discovered in Space*

HOT ROD

It's snowing dogwood blossoms this April Fools Day. Beneath the tree a 1949 Mercury coupe idles, hugging the curb. Angora dice dangle like square testicles from the rearview mirror. I'm walking by and thinking about fear, how it comes upon me as hunger, full of form and empty of substance, like now when the growl of unmuffled pipes on this classic car reminds me that I'm growing old. This is my fear today—that I've become an antique, past my prime and losing time. I need chrome added to my running boards, fender skirts to cover rust, and my hood buffed frequently or the color fades. My wide whitewalls are scuffed and require scrubbing with a stiff wire brush. Tune ups take more effort and newer tools. One plug is always fouled. This fear of aging is a small terror, I'm thinking as I turn the corner, when compared to my brother's, who has just learned he has lymphoma, or the horror hiding in the rest of the world as they balance their lives between cluster bombs and dysentery, malnutrition and malaria, river blindness and land mines. Still, it always catches me by surprise—the vague, but vicious, fact that even time, a concept without end, has its limits.

SONNET IN BEN THANS MARKETPLACE—
SAIGON, 2005

In the middle of morning glories and raw fish, an old soldier
with one plastic arm and air where another should be offers me
a package of postcards. If I buy them, he says he can help feed
his children today and I can show my friends I'm visiting Vietnam.
I tell him I was here in '68 before the truce, when he and I
were young men, when the grass grew high, watered with blood,
when his cracked teeth and my mind were whole, when we thought
there would always be enough rain for rice and wars served
a greater good, before we learned droughts, like bullets, come
and go without warning. He lays the postcard in my palm.
Metal clips click like real knuckles, warm with flesh, snap and pop,
release their load. But steel is cold and the curtain of pain
drawn across his black eyes tells me nothing of what this man
feels about losing the chance to ever caress his wife.

Jim McGarrah

LAST NIGHT AT
THE GIBSON COUNTY FAIR

On this hot night in 1936 nothing
was constant but humidity. Freckled
girls floated around the Ferris wheels
tied like helium balloons to the wrists
of future farmers. Blue smells of cotton candy,
bearing-grease, and rotted caramel apples draped
the midway in dim moonlight.
The black-toothed carnie cussed, spit,
and packed stuffed bears in boxes
while my dad waited for his dollar.

It was the first night he got paid to shill,
hustling money during that Great Depression
year to buy grandma's garden seeds
by throwing his best fastball against five milk bottles.
The balsa wood flew like frightened quail
and the carnie stacked lead bottles in their place.
Dad's friends lost their quarters and dimes.
Dad lost his friends and the hope that life
might be more than hustling spare change.
I know this story because I'm at my father's wake.

This tale isn't one dad confessed over beers.
He took pride in setting the right example.
The sin of survival carried in silence was a father's task.
But my uncle remembers, like he remembers
the tomatoes, cucumbers, corn, and cabbage
grandma grew with those expensive seeds,
like he remembers her hoeing the garden
in a cotton dress, bent over the wooden handle,
sweating in the dog day heat, smiling,
proud of her good son.

OPERATION LANCASTER, 1967

1

You notice the small things first,
the smell of Sterno-heated C rats, sweat-
rotted jungle boots, and dead water
in the rice paddies. The blanched sun
opens its mouth over the rubber trees
and swallows the last black bite of night.
The metallic trill of a jungle bird
you've never seen
hammers morning into your head
like a ten-penny nail.
Phuc Tran's rice wine still burns
through the roof of your mouth.
You haven't even raised
yourself from the hole you slept in
before a dragon fly whizzes by with a sound
like *why*, the single word, that one small word
that brings all these small things into focus
and makes the dawning greater
than the sum of its parts.

2

Death is buried where you piss and who knows
when the trembling wind will stop. Maybe
the mist foaming from the mourning earth
or the flesh-colored dust soaking through
your flak jacket will shield your heart and lungs
from the jagged burn of hot metal. Maybe not.

Small beige people glide by on bikes and scooters.
Some wave across the concertina wire
and you wave back as if the wire were not
an ocean, as if you might not have already drowned
them all in your numbed mind. That same sound
whizzes by, louder now than the dragon fly.

3

So motion is life, you think,
the fuel that fires your green age,
the clack of a rifle bolt
sliding home,
elephant grass churning
like the jade sea at China Beach,
the flutter of your butterfly heart
as it brushes against your ribcage,
the jangle of the wind chimes
on a sentry's watchtower
and the earth spinning so fast on its axis
that you get dizzy when Sergeant Williams
signals the patrol out past an old French
schoolhouse scarred by white phosphorus.

So motion breeds death, you think,
the force that shoves itself into your throat
from some ancient era of your back brain,
the uncontrollable twitch in your left eye,
and the slight palsy of your trigger hand.
You stutter in your step
as you push through the bamboo
to see the whirling point man deconstruct,
spun round, lifted up, pulled apart
by the mine beneath his feet.
You point and fire at shadows
till the shadows shoot back and screams
knead themselves into one long knot
of sound devoid of cause.

4

You caress your dead like baby birds fallen
from their nests too young to fly.
You bundle them gently into rubber bags
and tag their toes so families will know them.

But who knows the other dead?
Who cares enough to bury him,
a boy of twelve,
asking why he lies in a pool of brackish mud
stained orange with blood and urine.
Where is his ball glove and Yankees cap?
Who sees his parents shrink over an altar,
lighting sandalwood joss sticks, whispering
mantras that resurrect only smoke?

When you squeezed your trigger and the bullet
punched through the tight jungle air to touch
his chest, did you hope for his death
to be part of something bigger?
You still notice the small things first:
Sweat that stings your eyes while you wait
for the blue cloud of cigarette smoke to ignite
your lungs and a whisper like *why*
as the boy's last breath rushes past his small lips.

THE PURSUIT OF KNOWLEDGE

It begins by counting ceiling tiles during a lecture on fossils.
Semouria is a reptilomorph named for a town in Texas.
Winged lizards nested on the ground, unlike bats.
Straight-ankle thecodants evolved into crocodiles,
then humans.
I'm learning these facts because I want to become
a civilized man. In fact, I knew a thecodant
in Okinawa with perfect ankles.
Her neck smelled like jasmine and vanilla.
For an extra dollar, she whispered the name of my first love
when I climaxed. I think I chose Karen.

Anapsid, synapsids, and diapsids may have been warm blooded.

The professor's voice flutters along the walls,
a disconnected shadow in fluorescent light
and the girl sitting in the chair next to me is warm,
is no fossil. She smells like honeysuckle,
her hair, the laces of vines in my mind
that must be gently parted to reach a thought.
Her sighs distract me. They sound like spring rain
kissing a small lake.

Vocalization among different groups of dinosaurs
would strongly suggest some kind of social interaction.

Beside the blackboard, the professor chants his mantra.
I hear the NVA in the streets of Hue
during Tet of '68 before their immolation.
I can still smell the cordite and feel the heat
as we marched the tracer rounds up the pavement
in perfect cadence with the screams.

Jim McGarrah

Some cataclysmic event ended their reign over earth.
All we have left are fragments of their bones.

I'm learning to keep some knowledge from myself,
pretending, as it creeps back into my consciousness,
I'm someone else, an actor in a play
inspired by neither character nor plot as much
as the numb vacancy in my own voice and my skill at being
what I'm not, perfectly.

TRAVELING

Driving through Mississippi
in the 21st Century, there's nothing new
in my vision except a sign flashing through
the back-lit fog, a silent glossolalia of light that chases
small birds and sinners from the dangers of the neon night:
    JESUS…IS…WAITING
and so am I, for one small worm hole in this wall of gray air,
another galaxy for my restless mind, another woman
to replace the one I lost this morning in a hail
of frozen words and slammed doors. It's never easy
being a prick, but I've always been successful.

Too bad Jesus can't follow me
from His motel room of martyrdom, help me
find the inside of my heart where love wants to be
available always and by the hour. It's somewhere
in Biloxi this time, where the Dairy Queen sells beer
and fish factories ruin the bay with shrimp offal. We could
chase some tail along the beach and brawl our way through
nightclubs stuffed like sardine tins with servicemen.
What a sight—Jesus and me puking fried clams,
dry heaving like beached flounders, or pissing
up some brick wall behind the Waffle House.

Too bad…I see Him hanging in my rearview mirror,
a supernatural flame of fluorescent alphabet
disappearing around the next curve, replaced
by the faint outline of barbeque joints, tar paper
shacks, swamps, and rusted out trucks jacked up
on cinder blocks. I'm somewhere between Biloxi
and Hell in Rural Americana on a funky stretch
of highway that seems more memory than prophecy,

more a deju vu I've traveled through on the way
to someplace else *again*. Maybe Jesus knows why
the night is all that ever travels with me, how I picked
Biloxi when the land runs into ocean on a dozen
better beaches along the Gulf Coast, or why motion
keeps me still. If he does, he's not talking. All I hear
above the whine of warm night wind are clouds
as they scrape their tongues along the teeth of the moon.

DINNER AT LORENZO'S

A bow-tied waiter counts wine bottles in racks stacked strategically
behind the bar. Vines crawl along murals, light switches,
and spackled walls. Fresh bread bakes in the oven. Its scent kneads
into olive oil and oregano. Soft jazz trills in time with the ceiling fan
that needs a new bearing. A good Tuscan red sweeps across my tongue
like a velvet broom. I should be thrilled, but the limp of the glazed chef
carrying lamb as gently as a child lost to war, the absence of love
in a man's eyes when his hand closes over his lover's hand,
and the dazed smile of the hostess who wants to write pretty poems,
remind me that suffering idles in us all, a cosmic engine that torques
one scream above the howls of thousands, revved, waiting to rend
our helpless words into flayed shreds of desperate stardust. One breath
or a vague need slips it into gear. We all bear the drive like the taste
of this expensive meal, overcooked and doused with too much salt.

STUNNED

6am—sparrows gather.
Two ride a tree limb
above the cut bank
on the Wabash River, like boys
bouncing on a springboard,
ready to leap
into the brown current.
A third one dive bombs
the window I sit next to
and drink my coffee,
crashing downward, stunned
by the invisible glass
that blocks its progress.

This eventually happens
to us all,
our forward motion halted
by some unseen
impenetrable wall,
a tumor, a bullet, a driver
who drinks too much.

These days I fear
the fear
of being stunned
more than its certainty,
like the sheep paralyzed
by a lion's roar
long before the lion's presence.
It must be the process
of growing old. Once, I walked
into a thunderstorm. Drunk
and arrogant, I dared
the sky to crush me.
Lightning ripped a tree apart
nearby. Blinded,
I reached out
and pulled the lightning inside,
but I was young then.

Jim McGarrah

METAPHOR

"Rose is a rose is a rose is a rose"—Gertrude Stein

Or is it? The sign
on this table in the all-night Laundromat
reads, "I'm meant for dirty clothes."
But when the girl folding
her panties next to me, the one with a single
strand of saffron hair falling over her Botticelli
face, mutters the words out loud, an impression
hurls headlong into my psycho-sexual
shadow-life, like a shovel full of coal
tossed into the boiler
of a steam engine locomotive.

I digress.

The point is, the girl folding panties has
a rose tattooed on her left ankle
that is no rose. It's a thorny form
from red ink and translucent skin meant to transfer
                me to a world between soap suds and fantasies
                where flowers make love with dogs.

GUERNICA

What I don't remember is what I should,
that one day in April when a child plays
next to her mother's leg in the marketplace
of a small Basque town called Guernica.
She smells lilacs and mountain vetch,
newly tanned leather, coriander and cloves,
the hint of wine on the sausage vendor's breath.
All around her a warm breeze makes the pine trees
laugh, as the reds and blues of spring
buzz through the street in shapes of other children.
She has no idea what it means to be alive,
but feels a wild current surge through her arms and legs
as if she were the lightning rod on the schoolhouse roof
two hundred meters up the cobbled street.

When the Luftwaffe burns through the bright sky,
their engines humming softly, this girl has
no knowledge of her death. Giant steel birds
migrate to nest in her village. When they swoop
to tree top height she waves. The pilots smile back
and then open the bomb bay doors to drop their gift
of indiscriminant death. This is no brutal illusion
art creates, no future statement against the terror of war.
So, I force myself to think of paint,
like Picasso who sat alone in his studio, and I wonder why
he chose the absence of bright reds on his canvas, the angular
faces on broken bodies as they ascend in stunning silence,
the dead greens and grays for background, like fog rising
in a summer rain, offered to the useless sun.

Jim McGarrah

CODY'S DINER

Wind whines lyrically and the moon springs over clouds
like one of those round dots dancing off words of a sing-along song
on the Mitch Miller Show, the only TV my father watches, singing along

as if the barbershop quartet's harmony might cancel the struggle to sell
one more car to some farmer who's saved the first dollar he ever made from
Cargill Grain Elevator. Tonight, Dad's brought me to the diner for dinner.

I'm twelve years old, wondering if exhaustion will finally kill me after
chasing time for years, as if it were a mugger, down some dimly-lit corridor
between the cowering buildings that line State and Main in the center of town.

Will each step become more desperate to discover if the effort's worth
the cost? I see the question in my father's eyes as he reads the same menu
he's had memorized all my life and hear the fatigue as he orders two hot dogs,

faintly wishing I'd walk home to mom so he could slip around the corner,
enter Miller's Tavern, drink two martinis, or five, with the boys, play
gin rummy in the back room and talk about how the Cards should

climb from the cellar to win one pennant before he dies, one time, to prove
it can be done. Instead, we'll stay at Cody's Diner and he'll teach me how
to survive. The smell of his cigar smoke and Old Spice will fog my life

until I become a father and begin this process on my own. I'm talking
about wearing down from the friction of being the same person every day,
a drill bit bored in one beam of oak and then another until the metal frays.

ANGHIARI

James Wright might have laughed
at the irony here in Anghiari.
He was as fond of it as he was Italy
and this Tuscan village where he strayed
through the grass and studied spiders
the last days of his life. I don't know much
about spiders, but I like Wright's poetry.
When I cross the shadows
pushed through the Roman arch
by the sun's bronze hands, his spirit
seems to linger in this courtyard
beside St. Stephen's life-sized portrait
painted on the wall of a small chapel
connected to the village jail since 1483.

I would not compare Wright, or any of us
who write better than we live, to St. Stephen
as he fed the poor and begged mercy
for disbelievers. Which of us, as poets,
has courage to forgive our critics,
trust, like St. Stephen, that they stone us
for reasons preordained, grant them absolution,
and then through the process of our demise,
speak a language that yields
both love and blood, as roses do.
Poets are not saints. Wright knew this
when he came here inspecting spiders.
Saints choose life beyond language and then die for it.
We build our own prisons. We choose our own deaths.

Jim McGarrah

A NOTE TO LESLIE
FROM WASHINGTON PARK:

(West Village—New York City, 7/2000)

Years ago, daughter,
before the crack cocaine and the snarls came,
we played patty-cake sitting on this park bench.
I cradled you, like a puppy, between my elbow and palm.

We laughed with the rest of the warm world.
You nestled your head against the rhythm of my heart
as Euchre players chattered like grackles.
A flute, laced in a lattice of tambourines,
clicking Cuban heels, guitars in drop D tuning,
and one hollow bongo, reached to counterpoint
our harmony. These were melodies whose notes
sounded meaningless elsewhere.

Now, you've grown up, pink and pretty,
on your own in a world that sucks the marrow
from the bones of even its bravest warriors.
I'm watching the salmon-colored smog
swallow the Chrysler Building and thinking
I'll put the bulldog in your old room.
I made a bed in the empty closet,
so when her puppies are born, the illusion of beauty,
like this crimson sky, will comfort us all.

MARCH IS THE CRUELEST MONTH

Two robins and two jays trill
in counterpoint harmony as if Davis,
Coltrane, Parker, and Kirk flitted limb to limb
and spoke of various drugs and women
through the language of wind.

One leaf appears on a tree. You see it
through the bedroom window
and, like a caretaker in a cemetery,
sell yourself the illusion of rebirth
so you don't go crazy counting graves.

A woman is here and so are the stars,
full of cold fire lighting your mind
with memory and possibility.
The hooker on Tu Do Street
forty years ago with her silk *ao dai*

open to expose a thigh
the color of Tupelo honey reflected
these same stars from a different world.
You wonder briefly if that might be big
in some Jungian way, this woman lying so near

to your beating heart, a muscle you would
gladly tear from your chest and offer
as a mere token of what you feel,
like a ruby lifted from a velvet box, this woman
reminding you of how the past never

Jim McGarrah

escapes the present, instead of vice versa.
It's always the subtle things, sandalwood
incense, the hiss of the teakettle on the stove,
the flicker of shadows along the candle-lit walls,
that flash the rocket round through your mind.

Then the room on Tu Do becomes the rubble
of your life. The dust and the cordite take away
your breath and the woman who no longer is
bleeds into the one you lay beside and love.
Then, you bury your face in her hair,
smell lavender and fear.

THE LAST OF THE ROCK & ROLL POETS
PUTS A DOLLAR IN THE JUKEBOX

When Rilke couldn't write, he walked
through Paris in a fog until his muse found his memory.

Me? I listen for the same songs
played years later in different bars, like tonight,
reaching once more for those euphoric chord changes
only heard by youthful ears as my mind returns
to '67 when Morrison's lyrics entwined
with the wild scream of Vietnam and the swirl
of Jack Daniels invited me to grab
the girl across the table, giggle at her small
jokes, kiss her while glasses rolled off
shattering like gunshots against the floor.

If she sat by me now, I would share
this one thought: my life has always been
the same song played in different times, the same
journey down different paths toward her.

Instead, I'll drink and dream how our lips
might brush again, how this small
gesture might rescue me from absence,
inspire a new poem. I'll pretend
that what we both need has everything to do
with the melody in the air between us
and imagine I remember her name.

Jim McGarrah

THE MAN IN THE MOON

This morning as I drank my coffee, Henry Tauzin stood
swaying like saw grass in the jungle of my mind. The ebb

and flow of his body spilled over pale light until he became
my man in the moon, a myth born and breathing beneath banyans

as those trees dipped and swirled with the monsoon breeze.
The bamboo played a tango so hypnotic and hollow

I hardly noticed another whistle, the metallic trill
of an RPG ripping through the melody like off key fusion jazz.

Henry heard it coming though. He opened his arms wide,
embraced the blast to keep shrapnel from shattering my skull.

I caught his left arm in my lap, a beautiful Creole arm, tan
and ridged with sculpted muscle smoking like a sandalwood joss stick,

gathered the rest of him up and placed him in a body bag
as the moon surrendered all its promise to the numb shadows of dawn.

SUICIDE IN HIGH SCHOOL

Not all birds can fly and, while
this may be common knowledge
inside most aviaries,
I discovered the concept
one long night in '66.
My friend Sue perched like a bird
on the rail of Severn's Bridge,
dog-eared and faded copy
of the Tom Robbins' novel
Even Cowgirls Get the Blues
stuck behind her belt buckle.
She freed her white-knuckled grip
on the metal cross beams, spread
her arms and let the fringes
of her brown buckskin jacket
unfold like feathered wings. Then,
left the boundaries of earth,
rising just slightly at first
as if the light spring breeze might
lift her to orbit the stars
slung close to those cold girders.
We watched in awe, a small group
of classmates passing a joint.
Some cheered her amazing aplomb.
Others, myself included,
realized as she spiraled
into the river below
the absolute gravity
of believing all birds free
beyond the chains of the sky.

Jim McGarrah

ON LE LA STREET IN HUE, 1968 & 2005

You were a lucky package that came with this war,
like pound cake & peaches wrapped in C-rations on a good day.

The other marines outside the bunker didn't see your father
place an unlabeled box of condoms on the dirt floor or defiance
shading his black eyes as he surrendered your adolescence.

When my turn came I sold my watch to Marty Johnson for ten dollars,
market price for fresh flesh, and ticked off "I love you" in a brief stutter.

Now, each word has come undone, from wish to nightmare,
become the wet red bandana I placed across your eyes as propitiatory
blindness, a ransom sacrifice of sight for my shame.

Now, I've returned to Le La Street, stopped for white coffee
and to stare at the murals on this café wall. The jungle colors

rise in greens, browns, and yellows to reveal what hides
in the beige plaster—butterflies and naked children,
palm trees and elephant grass, rice paddies ringed in bamboo—

all some artist's optical illusion, like parts of you I see
mirrored in three young women leaning timidly on the bar.

Each girl hopes that I might wave her over, knows I would
tip well, has learned that my appearance in this place of ghosts
proves my pockets weigh heavy with guilt.

Each table holds a vase of fresh Cac Dang flowers and the floor
has been swept clean as if you expected my return.

AFTER GRADUATION, CHRISTEL GOES BACK TO VENEZUELA

We park before the brick and steel
of campus housing. My son and I load
the car with remnants Christel counts as life.

How slowly she finishes her sorting
through the scree of memory inside,
a copy of "Life" magazine with the Pope's
autographed picture on the cover, three combs,
perfume bottles, postcards from New York,
notebooks scratched with blue ink, and a white
wool sweater made in South America.

"This was a gift from my parents to help
me stay warm." She sobs and folds the fabric gently.
My son and I fight our impatience at this simple sentiment,
a metaphor for anima and, like tears, beyond the reach of two
males worried over traffic, airline schedules, and the need
to get somewhere on time at all cost.

This failure to surrender goal to process makes me sad.
I recall my father when he fed and bathed my mother
as if his efforts would convince some god of her innocence,
drive the illness from her twisted and terminal body,
and when it didn't, he died.

Jim McGarrah

A SONNET OF ABSENCE

My mother read romance novels
after we left home, hundreds of them.
Driven by absence beyond children,
she sat in her rocking chair, staring past
the empty nest into other people's dreams,
chain-smoking Virginia Slims
and mouthing out loud the clichéd language
her damaged hearing could not discern.
Ashes dripped from the cigarette
clenched between elegant fingers.
She was unaware that I sometimes watched
through the bay window before announcing
rare visits with a guilty knock. Unaware
that her body had begun to kill her, she knew
only loneliness and held it close like a lover.

ON THE 50TH ANNIVERSARY OF MURDER IN MONEY, MISSISSIPPI, DARK ENERGY IS DISCOVERED IN SPACE

Today, astronomers caught the universe expanding,
the density of dusk dancing with rhythmic energy,
whole galaxies split apart like diamonds. "No one knew

till now that the dark outside created light within,"
they said, as if this *dark energy* were a formless god
beyond our control, devoid of our influence, on fire.

Emmett Till learned the opposite fact fifty years ago
when he arrived in Money on the bus from Chicago
without the knowledge that traveling south would alter him,

make him into something less than human, without the cowed
deference that enslaved yet might have saved him. Two white men,
whose *dark* energy was born and growing inside light skin,

dragged Emmett to a river bank and beat blue his blackness.
Then, as if one death was not enough, they put a bullet
into his head and, with no remorse, went home to dinner.

BEING HUMAN

Four women sip beers
at Logan's Roadhouse this Friday night.
One I recognize in the neon lights
flashing on their wrinkled faces
as I crack peanuts open and wait
for some faux nachos to compliment
my fourth tequila. She's the nurse
that always warns me I drink too much,
smoke too much, weigh too much,
who must secretly hate me
because her husband died prematurely
from none of these excesses.
What if I'm wrong and the grimace
frozen like a smile on her face
as she waves at me and wags her finger
has more to do with living than it does
with dying, with going on each day
in search of some esoteric philosophy,
drug, or cacophony of religious noise
that drowns out this expectation
of how and when the end will come.
I visited my brother this morning,
after the doctor pinned his death
down to weeks, days, and hours,
even told him how it would occur.
I've never seen him more at peace, smiling
as we shopped for caskets like we did
his first new car, reflecting on the simple
clean lines, the sturdy undercarriage
and the thirty year, no-maintenance warranty.

FISHING

On the Missouri River, a skull-shaped sandstone cliff
holds two caves like eye sockets. Home to bears
and pirates, darkness in them feeds on liquid offerings.

Birch trees stripped by spring winds fence a cut bank
whittled by the whirling blade of a sharp current.
Purple moss paints the beach as if it were a canvas,

Picasso's latest, born from years of dying
in small increments until the numb and barren waste
brings the mimesis of art to life. My canoe carves

the stream while thoughts leap, silver and red,
in sunlight, a phenomenon of erratic poets
and dazed fishermen, or so says a faux friend

who teaches math in rubber boots. Rippled scars of water
sway the bobber, while beneath, many fish, one baited hook.

Jim McGarrah

A SOLDIER RETURNS HOME AFTER WAR

Nothing seems familiar here, as if I have gone too far
or not far enough. The ragtag apocalyptic howl
of a radio preacher becomes the hot empty wind
rushing through the pick up truck's open windows as I search
for landmarks on the same stretch of less urgent road I drove
a year ago to senior prom. The gas station has changed
color, the plumber hung new signs. The Smith's soybean field lies
fallow and their children play outside without watching where
they step, with no regard for helicopters overhead.
The sky seems blue, but that's illusion. Eyes filter light
to form nature's colors as my mind transfers memories
to my senses—the smell of burning oil poured on flesh,
the scream of cluster bombs and cloistered voices, the copper
jacketed taste of hot wind, the clammy touch of darkness
from a nameless shadow I feel constantly beside me—
my refuge of numbness, the dreadful bliss of arrival.

A VIETNAM VETERAN READS THE NAMES OF AMERICAN SOLDIERS KILLED IN THE IRAQI WAR—VETERANS' DAY, 2005

At first, it's about getting through an anonymous list—
Bill Jackson, Robert Johnson jr., Mike Jones, etc.—
and holding the microphone close enough to your lips
so the clang of barge bells on the river behind you don't
drown the syllables drifting like unmoored buoys
through the current of moist air in this commerce of life.

The sparse crowd bows a collective head, flags pop, traffic
hisses and slows beside the monument. In the middle of the list
syllables animate my past. Blood pumps through scrawled
letters as if loops and lines were blue veins. Names play baseball,
watch movies, walk hand in hand with teenaged lovers.
I'll never meet any of these men and yet I know them all,

perfect bodies ripped apart, reappearing for a moment, disappearing
whole in the blanched blankness of the turning page.

II

*Dark Energy Is Discovered
To Be the Source of Light*

PASSAGEWAY

(Vietnam, 2005)

Steam rises from red bricks, the dead
flesh of water resurrected.
Incense of fish and rotted wood leaks
from damaged crates loaded
at the Bason shipyard by splintered men.
Sweat claws my shirt and two destroyers glide,
like sharks, to dock beside a bonsai garden.

Un callejon sin salida—passageway
with no exit—a Spanish phrase
that might explain my memories,
except I'm not in Spain. I'm on a walkway
beside the Saigon River, slightly south
from Cholon. Moss streaks the water green
and blue as if some numb Impressionist slung
his pallet from one of the small sampans
moored next to a rusted freighter,
skipped it, like a flat stone, around the cut bank.

I stop walking for a cup of drip coffee
and 555's at a three-sided cigarette stall
where an old man dances with his granddaughter
as Billie Holliday's disembodied voice
—*God bless the child who's got her own*—
seeps from a turntable through the fog.
Spinning on his remaining leg,
wobbling like a top that decelerates
and gives in but will not quite fall,
he twirls around her, a whirling dervish
with the same urgent need for balance,
the same constant motion, the same
fear of slowing down that makes me feel
faint as I inhale the first blue cloud of smoke.

WHEN THE STARS GO DARK

There are no stars out tonight
in the alley behind Maidlow's liquor store.
Here, Charley Waters used to lean
against another old veteran of WWII
way back in the 60's when I'd come
down the block after high school
civics class and give him my allowance.
"You ain't old enough to drink," he'd say,
buying me a quart of Sterling beer and himself
a fifth of Thunderbird to quench his guilt.
They'd sip the wine, he and his buddy,
without saying a word, staring upward,
waiting for stars to pop through
the dusk like white kernels of kettle corn.

I'm in this alley decades later to piss
on the whitewashed wall and look
for those same stars. I've done it before,
bought bourbon and snuck out here
always to wonder, going to my car
as those blooms, some ice and some fire,
flowered somewhere in the distant darkness,
what Charley found in the vacuum
of the universe that caused
tears to swell in his blank eyes.

I almost had it once when I first came home
numb from Vietnam, a shadow in the primal brain
forming a vague shape,
gathering substance as it seeped
through me like hot tar,
that connection we've all had and lost
with our one beginning.

Jim McGarrah

Tonight, it's possible to imagine again
when all that's above me is a black
well of nothing hung on nothing.
What connects us is our loneliness
tearing through the endless sky,
arms outstretched begging the darkness
for a glimpse of those same stars
that always made Charley Waters cry.

TRAFFIC JAM ON HIGHWAY 41

Maybe it's because I miss my dog today, the mutt-bred one
that used to nuzzle my arm when we both needed a long walk,

the one the vet put down last Tuesday when her kidneys
quit working, or because the woman in the red Dodge

next lane over scolds the bare seat on her right, finger wagging,
head nodding, tongue lashing at no one, that I think of Carl Jung

explaining from the swirling midst of madness how all people
over thirty-five suffer from loss of religion, how we search

in unlikely places for nourishment to fill our empty,
aimless hearts, expanding roots along the desert floor of life

like the Joshua tree until we strike a patch of wet, lush soil,
suck it dry, and begin that same sycophantic crawl believing

there's somewhere useful left to get to. Yet, it could be what
Jung missed in his *creative illness* that keeps us all creeping

forward in this god-awful traffic, a homeless pair along
the highway's shoulder. The man, rose in hand, guides

the woman toward a vacant barn in hopes of romance.
She smiles, pleased to trade her deadened body for his concern.

Jim McGarrah

TWO LOVE POEMS

I

The Dancer
(for GC)

You should be able to write a love poem
even if you don't like the subject.
Language is all metaphor and rhetorical
meaning anyway. You can love
the idea of love without the consequence,
the image without ambivalence,
the prosody without pain, and even syntax
without fear of disease.
Syntax is order that creates rhythm.
You watch it now.
A dark and breathtaking woman glides
into the booth beside you at the Red Lounge
where you drink brandy. She reminds
you of Rilke's panther, dressed in black
and seething with primal energy.
Caged behind four empty bottles, her hands
pirouette in narrow circles the ritual ballet
of a spirit frozen by banal tasks
as she speaks of love and other necessary things.
Her muscles tense with each new sound,
the clink of glass, muffled laughter,
a nervous jukebox.
You feel their constriction in your chest
and wish you could paint her nude
with words, the almond of her flesh unleashed
and swirling with the rainbow of her body
in your mind across your page onto the essence
of this one word, love, that lives through layers,
like petals of a black orchid, in her humid eyes.

II
The Poet
(for VG)

A robin landed on the window sill this morning.
I thought it might be you.
You could never hide from me—
that slight tilt of head, those eyes
flaming like blue diamonds, and the song—
a siren-like sunlight chant through my open
window. You're a druid priestess whose heart
forms you into what others need. I would know you
as robin or wolf, Faery shaman or Cheshire cat,
frightened rabbit or Arabian mare cantering
through hot Saharan sands, ears pinned,
blond mane begging those long legs for speed.
So, when this morning you called to me as robin,
I flew over tulip trees and housetop
deep into that place Monet called vanishing point,
not caring what you were, only who.

ANNIVERSARY

Mom lays sockeye salmon
rolled in cracker crumbs
into a lake of hot lard as Saltines
swim along the cast iron skillet's shore.

She smiles at the browned flesh
of the burned fish my father hates
eating, but will as a small sacrifice
for his indiscretions with Beefeater's gin.

This is love: fifty years of marriage
without the sin of murder,
betrayal rationed by shot glass.
This is sacrifice: fifty years sharing
six rooms furnished with fear that one
might outlive the other and be left alone.

INHERITANCE

(a tourist's note to himself from the Balkans)

In an Adriatic Sea pebbled by spring breezes,
castles twice the age of your homeland rise from islands.
As the morning sun echoes off mossy stones,
you see into the past. Hapsburgs drink, cry, laugh,
and rule their way into oblivion while your ancestors
carve a raw wilderness into *The New World*.

Your soul's soul was born in this soil and its pearl skin
flushes red as you rage over Europe exploding
a few miles from your holiday in Trieste. Violence
swirls around the city, a constant flow of refugees
from Kosovo and the vapor trails of NATO jets across
the snow-capped Alps. A woman pushes a baby carriage

into a Kava bar and walks away to buy the morning paper.
Is she Serbian, Croatian, Muslim, or Christian?
Is the carriage wired with C-4?
Even in this beauty, this smell of salt air and diesel fuel, this taste
of calamari and Lasko beer, this roar of motor bikes,
the playfulness of gaudy fishing boats and old men mending nets,

this laughter of small children tied to their parents wrists and bouncing
like helium balloons along the crowded sidewalk—yes, even
in this splendor you can't stop thinking,
the only metaphor for life might be extinction. You wait
for the blast from the baby carriage that will lift the Kava bar
and its customers from earth, separating flesh from spirit

Jim McGarrah

by the sheer force of simple physics instead of rape camps
and ethnic cleansing practiced since the Roman occupation
two thousand years before. It never happens. She returns
with her newspaper and lifts the baby into her arms as you,
in your own brief history of napalm and Cruise missiles,
might lift a broken dream.

FREEDOM

When she's in heat, our dog Bugsy
can't be contained. I've pounded
fence posts three feet down in dirt,
surrounded them with concrete,
stapled the linked fence sections
to the ground, and piled brush
in strategic corners, only to find
grave-sized holes the next day.

Last Sunday, when I should have watched
the World Series, I dug a trench around
the fence perimeter and filled it with stones.
She learned to climb like a Nubian goat
before the seventh inning stretch
and escaped *over* the fence, searching
for one mystical bone buried
in some garbage can or compost heap
along State Street. Five neighbors
called and complained. A storm trail
of candy wrappers, soda cans, zip-loc
bags and tampon tubes lay strewn across
mangled flower beds.

Jim McGarrah

You'd think she'd look for love, her recurrent
condition being what it is. But every time I scold
her, the vacant gaze reminds me that getting laid
is just an empty ritual we all go through to cool
our blood when it begins to boil. The blue flame
that sears her brain when she runs unfettered
against the wind burns through every organ,
muscle, and instinct she has
pulling her toward the next block up the street,
the next fence, fire hydrant, bed of tulips,
the next chance to bark at the world
as if to say "You won't own me."

THE DEERHEAD TAVERN ON ORIGINAL SONGS ONLY NIGHT:

It was the clichéd poem-written-on-a-napkin night;
thoughts folded together like a spent squeeze box
in the smoke and foam, clink of glass, rattle and hum
of my worn mind, and then Emily's song opened
like a window broken by the casual toss
of sound through time and space.

Through the shattered frame, a chain of notes
spilled from her throat, rolling melodies
over table tops like unstrung pearls while I sat
lost between four friends and a glass of red wine.

Her wild vowels chilled and trimmed the air
communion-wafer thin. I bounced
between Goose Pond mountain in early autumn,
eating Key lime pie in Key West,
and dancing the *fais do do* on Canal Street as Cajuns
giggled, while the drunken moon
stared like a fish eye in a cirrus sea.

My body quivered along her guitar strings.
I made love to a Mexican girl under an arc of stars
in the Tuscon desert, swilled Guinness Stout
with Irish immigrants in Boston and then brawled
my way home as the sun blushed.

When the singing ended and a single strand
of yellow hair fell across her eye,
I felt silent again, but wrapped in a need
to laugh at myself,
to hear rain before it falls
and feel the breeze in a windless sky.

Jim McGarrah

NATIONAL ANTHEM

David writes the President once a month
ever since he walked, stoned outta his gourd, off Khe Sahn.
Swear-to-God, once every month, no matter who's President.

He hopes someone in the White House might remember
what could have been had we not stumbled on our own clichés,

trading handmade tie-dyes for MTV stock, swapping
vinyl records and beer bottles that pry open, for IPods, Blue Rays,
anthrax in the mail and malt beverages flavored with exotic fruits.

He *chooses* to ignore why we deal conscience,
like scrap metal, for corporate logos and Kalashnikov's.

Instead, David asks the President to replace
our Star-Spangled Banner with *Sugar Magnolia* and have
a marble statue of Jerry Garcia sculpted for the Rose Garden,

painted black and back-lit with a neon bulb flashing
—Gratefully Dead—twenty-four hours a day.

HOPPING A FREIGHT TRAIN

Forty years ago Jerry Miller tore
the wind in half. Arms pumping, legs churning
like pistons on the freight train he ran beside,
Jerry struggled along the tracks until that instant
when his need to do outraced his speed to do.
He flew toward an open boxcar
as the train switched gears, lost his balance
and slipped under a sextet of wheels, trading his foot
for legend in our local high school.

I'm standing where he started on a patch
of honey-combed gravel when the whistle sounds
a Charlie Parker wail over
the snare drum rattle of tracks and ties.
The Southern rounds the bend near my home.
I want to run with this train,
seek an open boxcar, like Jerry, and leap
headlong into darkness, even at the age of fifty.
I want to balance Jerry's failure against my own need,
that drumbeat in my brain that sounds like *don't give in*,
don't walk through a doorway while there's still a wall
to knock down, a woman left unloved, a city unseen.

My father used to say, "Oh, to be young again
and know what I know now." But, he sought
youth, even immortality. I'm no Ponce de Leon
in jogging shorts. I crave only to embrace,
for as long as possible, the unbearable ecstasy growling
in my throat when the challenge of the diesel draws near.

　　　　　　　　　　　　　　　　　　Jim McGarrah

MOROCCO, INDIANA

We're home to *Hoosier Hospitality* here.
The city sign says so. Even though
hardware stores, German taverns, grain co-ops,
Baptist churches, rusted tractors, and truck stops
long ago boarded their windows and stripped
their workable parts for spare change
to restart our out-sourced lives, we maintain
priorities by providing tourist necessities.

Our lone open store, which sells adult books
and Eveready batteries, unbolts its front door
each morning and leans against the cold shoulder
of the community graveyard. In Morocco, death
marries mindless sex with a series of ragged breaths
and the limp burial of hope. No questions asked.

TABLA ROSA

(my first philharmonic concert)

Rain drops
faster than rain.

A melody spreads like honey
                                        leaking
over my blank mind.

Stars explode.
Dust sifts through cello strings.

If life is melody willed by motion,
these walls breathe. They rise
and fall each time the conductor's arms flail the air
and resurrect the music Mozart died for.

If life is memory willed by senses,
I stand on Central Avenue in Jersey City
while its concrete fist unfurls in long fingers
of pool halls, warehouses and oyster bars.

                                        I stare

upward at a window where lost love

gazes back.

If this concerto is a white rose

it blooms
                                        tonight,

a token of lost gardens planted
years before I knew
all things beautiful grow alone.
In its thorns earth fuses and forms
forests and mountains.
Through its petals dawn drains
moonlight from lakes and the wind
spins seasons into symphonies
authored by a single cell.

CYCLES

It is a perfect day in the park as ten young men swirl
across the concrete court. Their foreheads bead with sweat,
breath leaking like steam from hot engines straining

to pull the weight of immortality up the long grade
of adolescence. My dogs tug their leashes, the crunching
paws scatter frost like dust over the last patches of summer grass.

They want that basketball the boys bounce with the same pure pain
that constricts my chest each time I see a hawk ride an air current,
a foal chase its mother's shadow across a timothy field, or children

smile at dawn and collapse the whole world upon itself.
Beside the park entrance, a small lake reflects a woman
dangling like a crazed and crippled puppet as she does

T'ai Chi and, without speaking, turns her flesh into the language
of air. I listen for meaning as the wind breaks the morning mist
over her outstretched arms and slows her down.

I am a boy again who lands the huge bass lurking
near the shore. I see the perfect rainbow sunlight scales
from silver fins when the fish rises, feel sweat leaking

in my palms as I crank the reel, hear crickets and frogs, how
the breeze lifts the limbs of willows and spreads their leaves
just as the line snaps and the fish flops back into the water

where it must still wait in the wet shadows for my return.

Jim McGarrah

GENERATION GAP REDUX

My friend Sarah confesses over coffee that she's a virgin,
but I can't tell from the tone of her voice whether it's brag
or complaint. She and her sister Rose think love
is related to lack of sexual activity, believing men
appreciate abstinence. But, Sarah's lover left her for the priesthood
and Rose eats Valium like M&M's when hers forgets to call.
Neither woman knew Susie, my first religion, the way
her auburn hair spilled over her left eye and brushed my bare chest
with cold heat, like snowflakes, while she read *Howl,* Ginsberg
propped playfully on my navel. "I don't think Allen ever blew Jack
as well as I do you," she always said. The contrast in her eyes between
pet cat and petulant child made me burn from inside out like the earth.
She kept nothing from our bipolar disorder called love until it exploded.
We entered that moment at the speed of light, and forever alone.

DIA DE MUERTOS

The First Death

When I die, I will be saved from death
by Mexicans. Each November strangers
who never saw me trip and tumble
over a crack in the sidewalk, heard me
curse another drunk on a crowded street,
smelled my cheap cigars, or touched
my scarred body, will eat candy skulls
and drink martinis in my honor.
Senoritas with rich black hair, who never
spoke with my ex-wives, will light copal
to ward off evil and then dance in my honor,
arms flailing like flowering vines
in the midnight wind, bodies shivering
at the hips in anticipation that I might
raise their skirts and kiss the sweet orchid
of their womanhood, like Roceria did as she
swayed in the bow of Miguel's boat
that one summer so long ago when I drove
to Acapulco and dove for conch shells.
Children will place the petals of orange
marigolds along a path from Saltillo
to Indiana that I may find my way back
to some sacred space they have reserved
for me where no senses are censured on the day
of the dead, except those most important,
the chance to feel once more, hot blood
drummed through pulsing veins and to gaze
with depth and weight into the eyes of love,
to have the space I fill regain its meaning.

Jim McGarrah

The Second Death

Hushed and solemn
voices will lower me past their black suits
into a world where mud is my only sky
and the earth holds me close like a mother might
clutch a soldier finally come home from war.
Out of my sight, their words will echo as laughter
at the end of a hollow pipe. They will smoke
cigarettes, toss roses on the loose dirt,
remind themselves of the time I saved a baby
from a burning building, carried my last cup
of water to a thirsty nun, gave someone
the shirt off my back, donated kidneys and lungs,
hearts and livers to the sick, bathed lepers
and, if not for my lust for women, might
have become pope. I would like to remain
in this limbo each November when boundaries
relax between their world and my dead one.
I am a better man where memory meets fantasy.

The Final Death

Memory is the devil that owns my soul
and when those who remember me die,
I will be put to rest.
On that day, no one lights incense for me.
Those left to drink and dance rejoice
for different ghosts who still take form
in the shadowed doorways of the mind.
On that day I will become the starling
I saw last winter trapped behind a great
window in the library where I sat
reading poems. The bird beat itself
senseless against the glass. Free space
trapped inside the frenzy of unattainable
flight drove it crazy until an old man
I didn't know threw a towel over its head,
lifted it gently and carried it out of sight.

Epitaph

My friend Ken studied philosophy,
read all the great masters and claimed
no stone could skip the surface of any lake
and not leave lasting evidence of its existence.

THE REED HOTEL

(for Rick Jackson)

Wallace Stevens slept here, although not well.
No doubt the traffic crawling down Market Street
and people chatting over coffee at the open air café
all night because their ante-bellum homes resemble
funeral parlors kept him awake in his Depressed era,
all that white noise, like lukewarm lava, flowing
backwards, sucked into the fire of his mind, stiffening
in the strophes of a misunderstood poem still unwritten.
I'm in the lobby of this ornate hotel, this last
bastion of Confederate pride with its white-coated black
valets and fresh cut magnolia blossoms, reading a note
some stranger slipped beneath my door while I dreamed
away the remnants of a French Bordeaux last night—
Dave, thanks for an unforgettable evening,
let's do it again soon. Love, Beth.

My name is Jim and, even drunk, I'm sure I would have
given Beth my right name. She seems like the perfect
candidate for my fifth wife, the way the letters in her note
curl and dip, the slight parting of words like whispered sighs,
the hint of jasmine drifting from lavender paper,
light and soft as a spring rain. I pretend for a moment
that I *am* Wallace Stevens, not just another crazed fan
of obscure but *resonant* imagery, as a girl standing beneath
the crystal chandelier, the girl in the blue dress,
red hair curled like a silk veil over her quiet, pearl-colored neck,
the one that could be Beth, stares at me. Wrought iron railings
and carved wood columns supporting the second floor
collapse beneath the weight of her brown eyes.
In the wreckage lies the language from that simple note.

READING SHARON OLDS

(for Matthew)

In one popular anthology placed neatly between
Frank O'Hara's and Mary Oliver's poems, a picture
of Sharon Olds resides as guardian of her own.
I like Sharon's poems, the way they get to the heart
of the bush without beating around it. But,
this morning I can't read them because I'm stuck
on the picture, excited in a way her words can't conjure,
the wide mouth with lips slightly parted, the challenge
of her stare as if she's telling me, "I know
what you're capable of and I like it." There's a certain
gray wisdom wound around the bitchy strands of
dark hair she combs off her forehead with the thin
teeth of her fingers. And, that long neck, the pale skin
translucent like a white orchid, the kind of neck
you could spend hours running your tongue along.

Once, while at a writer's conference,
two friends and I swam in a heated pool
the hotel let us use free for being weird looking poets,
as if the warm water would keep us satisfied in some
Freudian womb way and out of the bar,
safely separate from their normal guests.
Brett, Matt, and I floated in the shallows, white bellies up,
hung-over, frustrated language fish. We were middle-aged
men who resembled furniture movers, without the rep
to break lines the strange way Sharon could,
terrified that we had nothing more useful to discuss
than those simple enjambments in her best poems.

Jim McGarrah

The secret madness in Sharon's method
draws me to her photo this morning.
I love conflict between prosody and
physicality, the way words attempt beauty
when silence is the last best response in its presence.

THE ROPEWALK IN
NEW HARMONY, INDIANA

Two hundred years past, people in this utopia
made rope by walking, weaving hemp
as they stepped along a predetermined path.
Women in cotton dresses and sun bonnets
stretched fibers tight, crossed them over and under,
followed by their children, who wet each braid
for the summer heat to shrink the knots so tight
even Morgans could not fray the rope
as they pulled plows and broke dirt
into deep furrows to nestle the coming corn.
Standing on this path, I regret briefly not living
the life they led, giving my soul over to rain
and Christian salvation, self-sacrifice
and self-flagellation, plaiting the strands
of my history into a length of meaning more
than fleshly, until I remember the taste
of juniper berries in good gin, the single mole
in the small of my lover's back, the few poems
that came to me like fire in a canebrake, the smell
of dawn in the Catskill Mountains, the birth
of my children, the one racehorse I bet on
who got beat a nose, and last year's snowstorm in April.

Jim McGarrah

PEELING POTATOES

Numbness sprouts in fingertips and crawls up the forearm,
a Wandering Jew of monotonous veins, into the neck,
over the brain until you don't remember what you're doing, or why,
only that the task must be completed before synapses choke
the last few bored cells to death till all that remains is a scream.
This is similar to shopping at Wal-Mart or telemarketing.
You've done both in times of great personal crisis.
Once, when it seemed that your prostate had swollen
from lack of use, you did them together careening a crippled metal
shopping cart between rows of mouthwash and calamine lotion,
past bags of peat moss and fishing gear, motor oil and paper towels,
Timex watches and semi-precious wedding rings, across deserts
of ugly shirts and cat litter, talking all the time to a guy named Bill
on the cell phone about a free vacation at Disney World.

Sometimes, potato peelings clog the drain and things get thorny.
Your wife yells from the bedroom, "Call the plumber."
"I'll do it myself," you say and then borrow a snake from the neighbor,
with his assurance the flexible rod will cure any problem in five minutes.
Two hours later, soaked in sewage from the overflowing sink,
you grab the cell phone, drive to Wal-Mart and search for Draino
along with a set of earplugs, all the while philosophizing long distance
about wives and meaning in life to a guy from Bombay named Ravi Patel
who wants to sell you new tires for a golf cart you don't own.

Back at home, the mother-in-law sits in the kitchen
reminding the wife about the doctor she could have married, if only
she would have stayed in nursing school and not gained the extra weight.
You return to peeling potatoes, this time over a trash can where the brown rinds
spiral down and cover the refuse of life—coffee grounds, milk cartons,
newspapers, beer cans (you don't recycle), fish wrappers, tin foil, yogurt cups,
cereal boxes, a pack of Camels (you quit yesterday, but may dig them out soon),
a letter from Publisher's Clearing House saying you've won.

Suddenly, you remember Charles Simic's famous poem about shrimps
and wonder why you aren't smart enough to understand its deeper meaning.
Your wife and her mother grow silent until the paring knife slips,
sliding through skin on the right thumb as if it were a sautéed onion slice.
"Don't bleed on the floor. The dog will lick it up," they both say in unison.
Rinsing that thumb, you decide at last these spuds being slaughtered
are dreams trying not to die, wounded with water, starch, and dirt,
struggling to keep their skin, and then, diced to satisfy someone else's hunger.

ALTER IDEM

(Poetry Reading—the Balkans—2001)

We stood
one at a time
in various stages
of composition,
chanting
wild vowels
and consonants
as if the same
wool blanket woven
from different
languages might warm
us all, as if
smoke rising
in the room
might mingle
somewhere over
our heads,
signal us into the past
and remind us
that a few paved miles
ringed by mountains
were once all we had
between us,
not the ocean
of rhetoric
or the demagogues
that waged the wars,
or leftover landmines
that rip the legs and arms
from future generations
who may never
understand:

the first walls that must
come down
are ones bricked
with words.

A TRUCK FULL OF JESUS

A car's rear window carries Jesus
on the Lloyd Expressway at three
miles per hour over the limit.
I'm tailgating in my old Toyota,
staring at the beatific mosaic,
all halos and wings, all glazed eyes
and shattered countenance, all
heavenly exhaust fumes rising
like incense to shroud his face
in gray sorrow.

I inch my hood ornament closer
to the other back bumper, and pray
for proximity praise before my exit.

It happens—proximity praise,
blessings absent repentance.
Think of that one hungry beggar who
worked the crowd at what
he thought was a bar mitzvah
when Jesus fed the multitudes
with a few fish and still had leftovers,
the drunk who crashed the wedding
just as water changed into wine,
and Barabas, who escaped crucifixion
hidden between Jesus and Pilate.
Imagine Mary Magdalene's
paradisiacal payment when no one
in heaven ever asked for a hand job.

OLD HABITS

"Old habits die hard,"
my father would say as he filled
a Mason jar with ice and gin.
I remember him now, thirty years later,
apologizing to my mother that way.
I'm standing in the produce section
of a local market trying to find acorn squash.
A woman I went to school with caresses
tomatoes like they were her last hope
for one night of wild abandon,
existence infused with life. She has
no idea how often we used to make love
in my head or how, when we say hello,
my palms begin to sweat
and I still want to.

GROWING OLDER

Driving home from night shift on the line,
I shredded the right rear tire on a piece of glass.
The car bobbed and weaved like a drunk
confused by staggered
streetlamps. Treads unraveled.
It wasn't exactly a blowout,
just rubber rendered moot by wear,
dissipation tagged by a violent end.

The car trembled to a stop.
Younger tires hummed by
with the smooth sound of surf
on white sand. I knew I had a spare
in the trunk, one of those hard rubber
donuts that runs for miles and miles
at lower speeds as long as you don't mind
limping to somewhere close by.

My first real tires were white walls,
rolling on a red framed Schwinn—white streamers,
a wire basket, and no training wheels.
My father brought it home one summer
as if he finally understood
I had grown from him, but wasn't him.
It was our first step away from each other
and cost him a week's pay.
I'd give much more than that to start this trip over,
to find the bike and him both here today
leaning against my crippled car and worn-out tire.

THE RAM IN THE THICKET

I

Isaac

Sand swirls around the hem of his robe,
tents billowing in the distance like canvas sails
as he and Abraham trudge away from camp
toward Mt. Moriah.
The sun casts his father's long shadow
over the earth and shades desert cactus
in blackness. The boy smells their vanilla
blooms, feels their roots against
his sandal soles and wonders why his father
carts the wood for Yahweh's altar so far
from home, so close to desolation.
He asks as they climb into the clouds,
slipping on the damp rocks,
with the cries of carrion birds and jackals
in their ears, why no sacrificial lamb trails behind.
His father says they have a pact with God
and Isaac knows the heir's duty is obeisance.
He never questions why his father's
God might need his own youthful blood, or how much
land its shedding might buy for a people
not yet born, but stacks the kindling on the flat
plateau as Abraham glides his blade
along a whetstone and says, "Our duty
is to a thing unseen." His father's hollow
words will ring for generations of sons
and Isaac wants to cry, "How is that possible?"
Instead, he lets his father bind his hands
and lay him on the metal grate so blood
will drip and fuel the fire below.
Abraham places palm against sweating forehead,

Jim McGarrah

coaxes the throat to expose itself as if it were a white rose,
the bloom most beautiful right before it dies.
Isaac sees the knife slice through the thin mountain air,
the sun reflects his face off the metal,
the taste of copper fills his mouth when he bites his lip.
His heart thumps behind his eardrums so loud the clouds
tremble and throw their bodies against a graying sky.
What does death smell like—brackish water
in the salt sea, his mother Sarah's milkless breast,
and brother Ishmael's tainted flesh, all soaked
into the cuff of his father's wool robe as it drapes
across his eyes to blind the final stroke.

II
Abraham

Sunlight warms his olive cheeks as knowledge
of the promised kingdom warms his pockets.
Father and son climb the stone path.
Yahweh's voice drives them both
like sheep toward the summit, a wind
more word than air, a spirit unseen that powers
the father to think unspeakable thoughts
he could not bear unless his faith in God allowed him.
Through your seed, the nations of the earth
shall be blessed, through Isaac your descendants
shall be named. The voice echoes in his mind,
but he never questions how his son's slaughter
serves this purpose, his wife a hundred
years old, barren, and he so close to death the smell
of rotted earth and lilacs wake him every night.
Abraham knows only that to lead a great nation
father must be willing to sacrifice son.
He watches Isaac stack the wood, then binds
the boy's hands and lays him on the altar.
Sweat breaks along his brow as he guides
his blade across the whetstone. The sharp metal
shines and he wheezes in the thin air.
His mind begins to braid its dreams like rope,
generations into one strand—
Samson wrecks the Philistines,
David slays Goliath, the walls of Jericho tumble,
Mohammed screams *jihad*, King Richard
marches armies east for Christ,
heretics and flames, the smell of burned flesh,

Babylon built on blanched bones, a desert of red
sand spurting from the severed artery of the son's neck—
until the father sees one son is never enough for any god,
until he hears the harsh bleats of a billion rams
caught in eternal thickets.

LESBIAN SOX

When I was fifty years old I saw my first dildo
growing like a black cactus from the window sill
in Nickie's bedroom. It stared at me, malevolent.
I stared back inadequate.

"Does that thing hurt?" I whimpered.
"Not a bit," said Nick, "and it never ever says
it's done before I am." She had a point I couldn't argue.
Limp dicks are no fun and keen talk in the afterglow

often sounds like "Sorry baby, I have to go."
So why bother with the real thing
 if the illusion, like a Monet sunrise, brings you joy?
These things I understand, like why Nickie knitted me

a pair of yellow socks for a birthday present
instead of giving me a blow job. What confuses me is
all the fuss over sexual mores in a country
gone mad with mayhem.

Now I'm wondering why, as I pull up my sagging
yellow socks and head for the corner bar,
it's more Christian in my neighborhood
for a man to kill a man than kiss him.

Jim McGarrah

WHITE NOISE

I want the same cage that holds
a mime, a cell where bars are made of air
and the door opens like a pair of smooth legs.
Just once, I want Miss America to suck world
peace from a contest judge's cock, a cure
for both cancer and that infection of the mind
that keeps us small. Maybe a cigarette without guilt.

Yesterday, the river reached flood stage.
Brown banks disappeared beneath
brown water. Whitecaps ran, like feral children,
over sandbagged levees.
The hissing, churning, ripping, sucking undertow
sounds like all my thoughts today,

like how true horrors of war
both repel and attract. My friend Marty
found this out when he shot
an old Ba in Quang Tri while she slept
covered by grandkids and the scent of ginger
just to see what killing felt like. Then,
put the rifle under his own chin and slammed
a round through his cerebellum so he could find her
in some afterlife to apologize. I loved
that man for his refusal to suffer.

Once, no one,
not even women, connected sex
to making babies, or understood the difference
between cream pie and chocolate cake
lay more in texture than taste. But, today
I know trees live longer than humans,
that somewhere across town an old Jew davens,
waiting for her husband's ghost to explain
what the dead own.

THE USE OF LOVE IN THE POETIC LINE

How I have always failed to fall in love has more to do with humiliation
than fear of a broken heart, more to do with the Baltimore Hibiscus,
that Jimi Hendrix of flowers with long, flowing, red-veined fingers,

twangy in the wind and unwilling to grow unless left alone.
My concept of affection has more to do with Uriah Heep, burned-out
Sixties metal band, than Dickens' famous literary figure, or geese

being ill-disposed toward all other creatures while on the ground, yet
tolerant in the air. My lack of evolving warmth toward a long-term, fully
committed relationship bears comparison to Tod, a blue-eyed Jew

who paid his way through law school selling me speed and ended up a fat,
bald lawyer in the French Quarter fucking divorce clients of both genders.
Most recently, I failed to fall in love with a smart and beautiful woman

because of language. "The length of the poetic line is the only true
measure of a poet's penis," she said, as we sat drinking one of 67
kinds of draft beer in a faux German beer Haus near the Ohio River.

"I write poems
with very short lines," I quipped.

"My point, exactly."

Jim McGarrah

SOLDIER'S HEART

That's what Army surgeons called it
when Blue fought Gray, as if shooting your brother
was a romantic notion cloying, like honeysuckle,
in the ante bellum air. When the mortars
and gas filled the trenches of Europe
with sleepless nights and body parts, you were
shell-shocked, as if your mind were electric,
short-circuited by the surge of death around you.

Today, numbness has become
pragmatic and politically correct.
The new term is Post Traumatic Stress
Disorder, as if the mind were a deck of cards
stacked on the kitchen table waiting to be swatted
by a child's hand on the way to the cookie jar,
as if Freddie Johnson hadn't caught a bouncing betty
waist high like a handoff in a high school
football game, as if Billy Wolfe hadn't cut a penis
from an NVA soldier's body and stuffed it like an apple
in the dead mouth, as if Rick Santos hadn't eaten
his own bullet and left the back of his head all over
your new handmade in Hong Kong silk shirt, as if
limbless children and their faceless mothers
don't recoil through your brain every time some
asshole at a party yells incoming to see if you'll twitch.

Yeah, yeah…'Nam's been over thirty years, so quit
whining. There are new wars being fought, new labels
placed on old pain, new methods to fog memory.
Quit bitching. You're alive. That's more than you can say
for Phuc Tran and Phil Jansen, caught on opposite ends
of the same ambush the night you got your first clean kill.

Yeah, yeah…life goes on…suck it up…get real…it's in the past…
you know the clichés. You've got them memorized by now
and chant them like the mantra of that one Buddhist bonze
squatting in the market place at Gia Le, doused
with gasoline and trying to strike a match in the monsoon breeze.

EPILOGUE:

Peace

A small green fruit grows
only from the earth in Hue. Seeded
by the Trai Va tree, it rises round
and moist in soil blood-red with memories.

I share it now with my friend
Vo Que at the Garden Café
just off a dirt trail in this city where
my heart stopped singing
so many years ago, silenced
in a battle to claim what was never mine.

Que and I are two poets grown old
by sharing one dream from different worlds.

Here, in this jungle heat beneath lavender
blossoms and banyan trees that once shaded
tanks, rifles, mines, and death,
we speak of life. A voice within
us both chants in counterpoint harmony
beyond our separate tongues. Sometimes,
it makes the rustle of a spring rain,
the cry of geese in the gray dawn,
the whistle of wet wind through bamboo,
the drum of the Perfume River
beating ceaselessly on the stones of shore.
Sometimes, it whispers like a child's smile
or sunrise cracking a robin's egg sky.

I have traveled ten thousand miles,
decades through tormented time
and shattered space to hear
this voice rise within me once more,
to share a simple meal
with my friend, who, like the Trai Va,
no longer bears me malice for crimes
committed in my youth.

ABOUT THE AUTHOR

JIM MCGARRAH's first book of poems, *Running the Voodoo Down* won a book prize from Elixir Press in 2003. He has been nominated for a Pushcart Prize and a finalist twice in the James Hearst Poetry Contest. *Home Again: Essays and Memoirs from Indiana*, was published in August of 2006 by Indiana Historical Society Press and his novel, *Going Postal,* in April, 2007. A memoir entitled *A Temporary Sort of Peace,* which reflects his experiences as a combat Marine in Vietnam was published by Indiana Historical Society press in August, 2007. He holds a Master of Fine Arts in Writing from Vermont College and a Master of Arts in Liberal Studies from the University of Southern Indiana. He has worked as a janitor, horse trainer, carpet layer, mechanic, school teacher, hod carrier, hay baler, and recreational therapist. Occasionally, he drinks.